The Worldview Series

Your Living
Miracle

ALI NAJI

THE MAINSTAY
FOUNDATION

By: The Mainstay Foundation

© 2018 The Mainstay Foundation

Printed in the United States.

ISBN: 978-1943393381

In the name of *what is true*, including *what is right*, I offer the following attempt to the last *chosen one*. All blessed ones drink from that pure spring – some take only a sip while others quench their thirst perpetually.

CONTENTS

YOUR LIVING MIRACLE

Acknowledgements

In writing this short booklet, I considered including references to expert thinkers with relevant discussions branching off of the core ideas I invite the reader to reflect on. However, I decided that doing so would likely defeat the purpose of this publication. As a conscious reader will notice, although I discuss ideas that can be examined more closely by experts, I intently attempt to elucidate them in a way accessible to the non-expert.

Nevertheless, I realize the significance of being self-aware regarding the influence of multiple factors on my use of language, terms, categories and frameworks.[1] Although truth is out there for any sincere seeker, we seldom journey in a vacuum. For the ensuing reflections, I am thus indebted to various gracious souls, communities, and environments. First and foremost, I thank the truth for being there in a way that is accessible to some extent, regardless of all else. I thank my loving parents, supportive family and reliable friends, especially my beloved wife. I am forever grateful to my mentors and educators. Institutions and communities of learning across time and space command my lasting gratitude and reverence. I extend special appreciation to the Mainstay Foundation and its editorial team for supporting this project. To those I have neglected proper recognition and thanks, I cannot truly do you justice. As the wise have said, "How can I truly thank you when being able to say, 'thank you,' calls for another, 'thank you'?"[2] Any good in my work is yours and the shortcomings are all my own.

Your Living Miracle

When we cannot figure it out otherwise, a miracle is our proof that the person claiming to be a *chosen one* (or a *guardian*) speaks the truth. If the so-called "*chosen one*" is known to fall short of impeccable character and sound reasoning – based on fair standards – then such a person is not even a serious candidate. A *chosen one* (and a *guardian* as well, for that matter) is meant to be a lighthouse in word and in action, an untainted connection to *the one with no need*. Falling short of that purity disqualifies any potential claimant. If claimant X says [s]he is the creator of *the one with no need*, our sound reasoning can expose such a charlatan right off the bat. The same goes for any other with an absurd claim. *The one with no need* is beyond all needs, limitations and deficiencies. *The one with no need* creates but is not created. He creates physical boundaries for things but is never bounded by them. Furthermore, if claimant Y is known to be a liar or a cheat, our common sense suffices to discover that deceit. Even if those crooked claimants can put on a spectacle – illusions, magic tricks, predictions, and the like – their flawed character and/or claims show us how far they are from the light.

However, if claimant Z is a real candidate – with a plausible claim and upright character along with it – then a miracle can certify that the puzzle pieces fit. For *the one with no need* would not leave us to be misguided by a feat without giving us a means to reveal the deception. The introduction of *a challenge to the natural order* is proof that *the one with no need* is the approver and awarder. If this claimant Z can bring forth a valid miracle, then we can be sure that such a claim is veridical. Not every miracle has to be exactly the same – every rose has a fragrance and each person has a name. The type of miracle is dictated by *the one with no need*, while the *chosen one* serves to deliver the message as decreed. Finally, miracles are exceptional and occur when necessary – they are not meant to eliminate agency and keep us stationary.

Don't Look Back in Time Yet

Where do we look for a miracle? Must we look back in time? Are there no miracles accessible to us in our present? One way of looking for a miracle is to figure out a way to establish that, "Once upon a time, miracle X happened." How would we go about doing that? *Presumably, the same way we would go about proving the credibility of any narrative in history.* Personal and collective memories contribute to our confidence about what happened in the past, at least to some extent. But as we might expect, sometimes memories may be skewed or selective. Controversial incidents may be "remembered" in different ways by rivaling groups. Some painful incidents may not be passed down with all their hurtful details. Humiliating defeats may be sugar-coated. Victories might be exaggerated, and so forth. Each of us might already realize how this goes for the recent past, let alone the distant past. Therefore, relying on memory alone does not always make us *sure* of what happened in the past.

Granted, memory might be enough in some cases. The quantity and/or quality of individuals "remembering" for generations back may be so profound that I am *sure* they would not *all* conspire to tell a lie or *collectively* misinterpret what happened. How so? Well, maybe because these are people known to be honest members of their communities. Or maybe they are from different regions, but all confirming the same basic storyline. One way or another, the characteristics and numbers of these individuals makes me sure they would not collude to tell a lie. Moreover, their narrative may be consistent with what I would have expected in light of other things that I know (e.g. my anticipation that the *one with no need* surely appoints *chosen ones* to guide humanity and that the last *chosen one* must have appointed an impeccable *guardian* to guard the final "software update").[3] These and similar factors may very well make me sure about key events – even in the distant past. The agreement of rivaling groups might also have bearing in this regard, and so would the nature of the claim at stake. If these factors fail, as far as memory goes, then documentary evidence, archeological evidence, textual analysis, inter-textual references, and other forms of evidence might come to the rescue. Finally, since *the one with no need* would surely safeguard a threshold of truth for humans seeking guidance through *chosen ones* and *guardians*, there must be a surviving narrative that leads down that path. The core truth would be defended rigorously, intellectually and physically, and its people would not simply die out. In other words, by process of elimination, one of the surviving basic narratives must be true.[4]

But what if that didn't work for you or me? What if we tried our best and still could not become sure that any supposed "miracle" actually occurred in the past? What if we simply failed to become convinced that Moses split the sea or that Jesus raised the dead? Not because we are stubborn or unreasonable, not because we are unwilling to open our eyes or our hearts, not because we are reluctant to step up to the plate of responsibility… but because we don't find the evidence convincing. Are we doomed because we attempt to look back in time? Better yet, even if we *are* convinced about miracles in the distant past, what about now? Are there any miracles that survive till this day? There have been so many claimants in history. Which "software" works best to maximize humanity's guidance and safeguard the journey toward eternity? Do they all even *work*? Which supposed "*chosen one*" is really speaking on behalf of *the one with no need*? Is there a final *chosen one* with the most updated "software"? Is there any miracle that we can lay our hands on *today*? What is your living miracle?

A Miracle in Words?

There *is* a living miracle claim for us to consider. It has an open challenge for all of humanity. It claims to use the letters of a human alphabet in ways that challenge the natural order of things. In its eloquent language, in its profound concepts, in its peculiarly precise descriptions and foresight, in its sheer irreproducibility, it claims to be proof from *the one with no need*. It speaks with the certainty that only special permission from *the one with no need* could give way to its unique character. In this sense, no less of a challenge than splitting the sea or raising the dead, it claims to present the best of guidance with dimensions transcending the natural order.

It is a recitation written down in the form of chapters. Some of its verses are straightforward while others require closer examination and may require interpretation. It calls itself the *recitation* (Qur'ān), definitively stating that it is an unrivaled sign from God. As a living challenge to both humans and alien creatures, the Qur'ān states,

قُل لَّئِنِ اجتَمَعَتِ الإِنسُ وَالجِنُّ عَلَى أَن يَأْتُوا بِمِثلِ هٰذَا القُرآنِ لا يَأْتُونَ بِمِثلِهِ وَلَو كَانَ بَعضُهُم لِبَعضٍ ظَهِيرًا

Say, 'Should all humans and jinn rally to bring the like of this Qur'ān, they will not bring the like of it, even if they assisted one another.' [5, 6]

It is a book that was compiled around 14 centuries ago, as confirmed by generations of peoples who memorized and transcribed it across the globe, carbon dating of extant manuscripts, and other evidence. This is none other than the book associated with Muhammad, the *chosen one* of Islam. If language experts had been able to meet the Qur'ān's challenge, then their work would have gone down in history, surviving to our present, as a rival to the celebrated Qur'ān. Had there been a serious competitor to the Qur'ān's challenge, its ripples would be felt today, somehow, somewhere. But such a rival is nowhere to be found. Instead, we find that the Qur'ān's influence continues to grow as new dimensions of its miracle come to light. Indeed, it is not *only* the Qur'ān's challenge in Arabic eloquence that has proffered its prominence today. The Qur'ān won on that front long ago. One of the most intriguing aspects of the Qur'ān for today's reader is how it contains precise descriptions of scientific realities – long before they were known to humanity...

Precise Descriptions

The Qur'ān is not a book on science per se. It claims to be the book of supreme guidance, as I will describe later. But several verses in the Qur'ān are far too precise in their wording regarding sci-

entific realities than to be dismissed as coinci-
dental. Thus, the reader today has a new layer of
Qur'ānic wonder to reflect on in light of recent scientific discoveries. The Qur'ān says,

أَوَلَم يَرَ الَّذينَ كَفَروا أَنَّ السَّماواتِ وَالأَرضَ كانَتا رَتقًا
فَفَتَقناهُماۖ وَجَعَلنا مِنَ الماءِ كُلَّ شَيءٍ حَيٍّۖ أَفَلا يُؤمِنونَ

*Have the faithless not regarded that the
heavens and the earth were interwoven
and We unravelled them, and We made
every living thing out of water? Will they
not then have faith?[7]*

Is the Qur'ān pointing to scientific facts that humans have only discovered recently? Were the
heavens and the earth once a single mass that was
then parted? Isn't the Qur'ān apparently pointing
to a deep connection between water and all bio-
logical life? In another verse, the Qur'ān says,

وَالسَّماءَ بَنَيناها بِأَيدٍ وَإِنّا لَموسِعونَ

*We have built the sky with might, and in-
deed it is We who are expanding it.[8]*

For a reader today, does this not sound surprisingly reminiscent of recent scientific discovery about the expanding universe? Is this a hint from "Allah" (the Arabic name for God, *the one with no need*) left for later readers – like us today – to appreciate? In yet another verse, we read,

وَتَرَى الْجِبَالَ تَحْسَبُهَا جَامِدَةً وَهِيَ تَمُرُّ مَرَّ السَّحَابِ
صُنْعَ اللَّهِ الَّذِي أَتْقَنَ كُلَّ شَيْءٍ ۚ إِنَّهُ خَبِيرٌ بِمَا تَفْعَلُونَ

And you see the mountains, which you suppose to be stationary, while they drift like passing clouds —the handiwork of God who has made everything faultless. He is indeed well aware of what you do.[9]

Is the Qurʾān hinting to its readers – today – that it knew the Earth was in motion even when people thought it was stationary? The early readers of the Qurʾān may not have realized the precision in this verse's description, but a reader today does not have to read much into it to realize such precision. There are many other examples and the reader is invited to examine the Qurʾān's miraculous dimensions more closely. Only time will tell what additional wonders will become apparent to readers of the Qur'ān in the future. As the Qur'ān promises, inspiring us to contemplate,

سَنُرِيهِم آيَاتِنا فِي الآفاقِ وَفِي أَنفُسِهِم حَتَّىٰ يَتَبَيَّنَ لَهُم أَنَّهُ الحَقُّ ۗ أَوَلَم يَكفِ بِرَبِّكَ أَنَّهُ عَلىٰ كُلِّ شَيءٍ شَهِيدٌ

Soon We shall show them Our signs in the horizons and in their own souls until it becomes clear to them that [it] is the truth. Is it not sufficient that your Lord is witness to all things?[10]

Holistic Guidance

The Qur'ān's formidable challenge is in its roadmap for holistic guidance. This book claims to be a guide for individuals and communities, including all the necessary elements for guidance – historical, educational, legislative, expressive, etc. In the Qur'ān, we read,

إِنَّ هٰذَا القُرآنَ يَهدي لِلَّتي هِيَ أَقوَمُ وَيُبَشِّرُ المُؤمِنينَ
الَّذينَ يَعمَلونَ الصّالِحاتِ أَنَّ لَهُم أَجرًا كَبيرًا

Indeed this Qur'ān guides to what is most upright, and gives the good news to the faithful who do righteous deeds that there is a great reward for them.[11]

Each reader is, thus, invited to study the Qur'ān and evaluate its word from the perspective [s]he can surely discern right from wrong in. Today's thinkers, scientists, and even the general public are summoned to either meet the Qur'ānic challenge or accept the truth. Does the Qur'ān ever err? Does any approach match that of the Qur'ān when the bigger picture is taken into account? Can any human endeavor produce the like of the Qur'ān's comprehensive program for mind, body and soul? The Qur'ān has continued to trump every attempt to undermine it. For those who still remain skeptical about the author of the Qur'ān's "*sūrahs*" (chapters), the Qur'ān records another challenge,

أَم يَقولونَ افتَراهُ ۖ قُل فَأتوا بِعَشرِ سُوَرٍ مِثلِهِ مُفتَرَياتٍ وَادعوا مَنِ استَطَعتُم مِن دونِ اللَّهِ إِن كُنتُم صادِقينَ. فَإِلَّم يَستَجيبوا لَكُم فَاعلَموا أَنَّما أُنزِلَ بِعلمِ اللَّهِ وَأَن لا إِلَٰهَ إِلّا هُوَ ۖ فَهَل أَنتُم مُسلِمونَ

Do they say, 'He has fabricated it?' Say, 'Then bring ten sūrahs like it, fabricated, and invoke whomever you can, besides God, should you be truthful.' But if they do not respond to you, know that it has been sent down by God's knowledge, and that there is no god except Him. Will you, then, submit [to God]?[12]

Ten chapters… That's all it would take. If people could produce even ten chapters like the chapters of the Qur'ān, then the Qur'ān would not be miraculous. But reality wakes us up from the slumber of such a fantasy today – there are no serious contenders. The Qur'ān pushes the challenge further, claiming that even a single one of its chapters is beyond human replication,

أَم يَقُولُونَ افْتَرَاهُ قُل فَأْتُوا بِسُورَةٍ مِثْلِهِ وَادعوا مَنِ استَطَعتُم مِن دونِ اللَّهِ إِن كُنتُم صادِقينَ

Do they say, 'He has fabricated it?' Say, 'Then bring a sūrah like it, and invoke whomever you can, besides God, should you be truthful.'[13]

The one with no need would not allow a liar to access the realm of miraculous power. If we do establish a miracle, therefore, then it is proof that a potential candidate is telling the truth. Unless we know the claimant to be fraudulent, we have no reasonable choice but to submit that the miracle attests to the claimant's authenticity.

The Last Chosen One

Your living miracle, the Qur'ān, speaks of the present during which it was first revealed. It points to a *chosen one* of extraordinary character. When it speaks to us, it tells us,

لَقَد كَانَ لَكُم في رَسولِ اللَّهِ أُسوَةٌ حَسَنَةٌ لِمَن كَانَ يَرجُو اللَّهَ وَاليَومَ الآخِرَ وَذَكَرَ اللَّهَ كَثيرًا

In the Messenger of God there is certainly for you a beautiful exemplar – for those who look forward to God and the Last Day, and remember God greatly.[14]

The Qur'ān addresses Muhammad directly, as if it is inviting our reflective attention,

$$وَإِنَّكَ لَعَلَىٰ خُلُقٍ عَظِيمٍ$$

And indeed you are of an exalted charac-ter.[15]

The Qur'ān has survived the centuries to testify for Muhammad as the final *chosen one*. The narrative of over a billion human beings on Earth today is confirmed by this living miracle,

ما كانَ مُحَمَّدٌ أَبا أَحَدٍ مِن رِجالِكُم وَلَكِن رَسولَ اللَّهِ وَخاتَمَ النَّبِيِّينَ ۗ وَكانَ اللَّهُ بِكُلِّ شَيءٍ عَليمًا. يا أَيُّهَا الَّذينَ آمَنُوا اذكُرُوا اللَّهَ ذِكرًا كَثيرًا. وَسَبِّحوهُ بُكرَةً وَأَصيلًا. هُوَ الَّذي يُصَلّي عَلَيكُم وَمَلائِكَتُهُ لِيُخرِجَكُم مِنَ الظُّلُماتِ إِلَى النّورِ ۚ وَكانَ بِالمُؤمِنينَ رَحيمًا. تَحِيَّتُهُم يَومَ يَلقَونَهُ سَلامٌ ۚ وَأَعَدَّ لَهُم أَجرًا كَريمًا. يا أَيُّهَا النَّبِيُّ إِنّا أَرسَلناكَ شاهِدًا وَمُبَشِّرًا وَنَذيرًا. وَداعِيًا إِلَى اللَّهِ بِإِذنِهِ وَسِراجًا مُنيرًا. وَبَشِّرِ المُؤمِنينَ بِأَنَّ لَهُم مِنَ اللَّهِ فَضلًا كَبيرًا. وَلا

تُطِعِ الكافِرِينَ وَالمُنافِقِينَ وَدَع أَذاهُم وَتَوَكَّل عَلَى اللَّهِ ۚ وَكَفىٰ بِاللَّهِ وَكِيلًا.

Muḥammad is not the father of any man among you, but he is the Messenger of God and the Seal of the Prophets, and God has knowledge of all things. O you who have faith! Remember God with frequent re-membrance, and glorify Him morning and evening. It is He who blesses you, and so do His angels, that He may bring you out from darkness into light, and He is most merciful to the faithful. The day they encounter Him, their greeting will be, 'Peace,' and He holds in store for them a noble reward. O Prophet! Indeed We have sent you as a wit-ness, as a bearer of good news and as a warner; and as an inviter unto God by His permission, and as a radiant lamp. An-nounce to the faithful the good news that there will be for them a great grace from God. And do not obey the faithless and the hypocrites, and disregard their torments,

and put your trust in God, and God suffices
as trustee.[16]

The Qur'ān speaks of the *Seal of All Prophets*, the last *chosen one*, the unschooled man starting out from *Umm al-Qura* (otherwise known as Mecca). He is a man not known to have read or written before the revelation of this Qur'ān,

$$\text{وَما كُنتَ تَتلو مِن قَبلِهِ مِن كِتابٍ وَلا تَخُطُّهُ بِيَمينِكَ}$$
$$\text{إِذًا لَارتابَ المُبطِلونَ}$$

You did not use to recite any scripture be-
fore it, nor did you write it with your right
hand, for then those who make false claims
would have been skeptical.[17]

Nevertheless, the Qur'ān describes him as one with unique access to knowledge from *the one with no need* – it is *chosen-one* revelation,

$$\text{ما ضَلَّ صاحِبُكُم وَما غَوىٰ. وَما يَنطِقُ عَنِ الهَوىٰ. إِن}$$
$$\text{هُوَ إِلّا وَحيٌ يوحىٰ}$$

*Your companion[18] has neither gone astray,
nor gone amiss. Nor does he speak out of
[his own] desire: it is just a revelation that
is revealed [to him][19]*

He is a messenger calling toward moral action, at heart and in deed. Those who accept the truth in his message and follow it faithfully open up to distinct mercy and success,

الَّذِينَ يَتَّبِعونَ الرَّسولَ النَّبِيَّ الأُمِّيَّ الَّذي يَجِدونَهُ مَكتوبًا عِندَهُم في التَّوراةِ وَالإِنجيلِ يَأْمُرُهُم بِالمَعروفِ وَيَنهاهُم عَنِ المُنكَرِ وَيُحِلُّ لَهُمُ الطَّيِّباتِ وَيُحَرِّمُ عَلَيهِمُ الخَبائِثَ وَيَضَعُ عَنهُم إِصرَهُم وَالأَغلالَ الَّتي كانَت عَلَيهِم ۚ فَالَّذينَ آمَنوا بِهِ وَعَزَّروهُ وَنَصَروهُ وَاتَّبَعُوا النّورَ الَّذي أُنزِلَ مَعَهُ ۙ أُولٰئِكَ هُمُ المُفلِحونَ

—those who follow the Messenger, the unschooled prophet, whose mention they find written with them in the Torah and the Evangel, who bids them to do what is right and forbids them from what is wrong,

makes lawful to them all the good things and forbids them from all vicious things, and relieves them of their burdens and the shackles that were upon them —those who believe in him, honor him, and help him and follow the light that has been sent down with him, they are the felicitous.'[20]

The prophecies from previous *chosen ones* would have referred to the last *chosen one*, either by name, by unique qualities, or both. Readers interested in that approach to knowing the last *chosen one* and the *guardians* of his message should consult the previous revealed scriptures in their original languages.[21] In any case, the miracle of the Qur'ān offers proof for all those anticipating a *chosen one* – those affiliated with previous *chosen ones*, such as Moses and Jesus, as well as others. As for Muhammad, being sent to Mecca is only the beginning. The Qur'ān describes the last *chosen one* as a messenger to the entirety of humanity,

وَما أَرسَلناكَ إِلّا كافَّةً لِلنّاسِ بَشيرًا وَنَذيرًا وَلٰكِنَّ أَكثَرَ

النّاسِ لا يَعلَمونَ

We did not send you except as a bearer of good news and warner to all mankind, but most people do not know.[22]

In a sense, perhaps even more encompassing, *the one with no need* addresses Muhammad as a conduit of mercy with universal dimensions,

$$وَما أَرسَلناكَ إِلّا رَحمَةً لِلعالَمينَ$$

We did not send you but as a mercy to all the worlds.[23]

The *one with no need* shows us the path of love by inviting us to follow in the footsteps of the last *chosen one*,

$$قُل إِن كُنتُم تُحِبّونَ اللَّهَ فَاتَّبِعوني يُحبِبكُمُ اللَّهُ وَيَغفِر لَكُم ذُنوبَكُم ۗ وَاللَّهُ غَفورٌ رَحيمٌ$$

Say, 'If you love God, then follow me; God will love you and forgive you your sins, and God is all-forgiving, all-merciful.'[24]

It is about love for the One and Only, who is *independently* excellent beyond any limitation – *the one with no need*. The Qur'ān reminds us of our need for God when it touches us, saying,

يَا أَيُّهَا النَّاسُ أَنتُمُ الْفُقَرَاءُ إِلَى اللَّهِ ۖ وَاللَّهُ هُوَ الْغَنِيُّ الْحَمِيدُ

O mankind! You are the ones who stand in need of God, and God—He is the Self-Sufficient, the All-laudable.[25]

As if the entire message is meant to draw us toward that fountain of life, *the one with no need* invites us,

يَا أَيُّهَا الَّذِينَ آمَنُوا اسْتَجِيبُوا لِلَّهِ وَلِلرَّسُولِ إِذَا دَعَاكُم لِمَا يُحْيِيكُمْ ۖ وَاعْلَمُوا أَنَّ اللَّهَ يَحُولُ بَيْنَ الْمَرْءِ وَقَلْبِهِ وَأَنَّهُ إِلَيْهِ تُحْشَرُونَ

O you who have faith! Answer God and the Messenger when he summons you to that which will give you life. Know that God intervenes between a man and his heart and that toward Him you will be gathered.[26]

This is the invitation that brings us life. God has nothing to gain from us, for God is *the one with no need*. It is through the revelation from God that *we* can achieve *our* purpose and come closer to the greatest reality of excellence, *the one with no need*, God Almighty. In this vein, then, God gives us an unequivocal prescription to express our love by following the last *chosen one's* guidance,

قُل أَطِيعُوا اللَّهَ وَأَطِيعُوا الرَّسولَ ۖ فَإِن تَوَلَّوا فَإِنَّمَا عَلَيهِ ما حُمِّلَ وَعَلَيكُم ما حُمِّلتُم ۖ وَإِن تُطِيعوهُ تَهتَدوا ۚ وَما عَلَى الرَّسولِ إِلَّا البَلاغُ المُبينُ

Say, 'Obey God, and obey the Messenger.' But if you turn your backs, [you should know that] he is only responsible for his burden and you are responsible for your burden, and if you obey him, you shall be guided, and the Messenger's duty is only to communicate in clear terms.[27]

Guidance comes to us from God when we answer the call of the Messenger – the *chosen one*, as we have referred to him throughout these booklets.

These verses open us up not only to the revelation manifest in the Qur'ān but also to the walking, talking revelation in the very person of Muhammad. If we can, then, establish that the last *chosen one* said or did something, those words and actions also represent the way of life (*sunnah*) for us to follow.

The 12 Guardians

Hence, the *verified* reports about Muhammad's words and actions, passed down generation after generation, become critically relevant. But God knows, as does the Messenger, that ordinary people might fail to guard the message properly – they may even turn back on their heels. As the Qur'ān inquires,

وَما مُحَمَّدٌ إِلّا رَسُولٌ قَد خَلَت مِن قَبلِهِ الرُّسُلُ ۚ أَفَإِن ماتَ أَو قُتِلَ انقَلَبتُم عَلىٰ أَعقابِكُم ۚ وَمَن يَنقَلِب عَلىٰ عَقِبَيهِ فَلَن يَضُرَّ اللَّهَ شَيئًا ۗ وَسَيَجزِي اللَّهُ الشّاكِرينَ

Muhammad is but a Messenger; [other] Messengers have passed before him. If he dies or is slain, will you turn back on your heels? Anyone who turns back on his heels will not harm God in the least, and God will reward the grateful.[28]

For this reason and others, God provides fail-safe *guardians* of the Messenger's guidance for us to follow. They are *guardians* of God's message, as delivered by the Messenger, the last *chosen one*. The Qur'ān invites those who love God to defer matters of guidance back to God and the Messenger by following these *guardians* just as they would follow the Messenger,

يا أَيُّهَا الَّذينَ آمَنوا أَطيعُوا اللَّهَ وَأَطيعُوا الرَّسولَ وَأُولي الأَمرِ مِنكُم ۖ فَإِن تَنازَعتُم في شَيءٍ فَرُدّوهُ إِلَى اللَّهِ وَالرَّسولِ إِن كُنتُم تُؤمِنونَ بِاللَّهِ وَاليَومِ الآخِرِ ۚ ذٰلِكَ خَيرٌ وَأَحسَنُ تَأويلًا

O you who have faith! Obey God and obey the Messenger and those vested with authority among you. And if you dispute concerning anything, refer it to God and the Messenger, if you have faith in God and the Last Day. That is better and more favorable in outcome.[29]

The community that takes these appointed *guardians*, "those vested with authority," as its divinely selected *Imams* is holding on to the way of Muhammad. After the last *chosen one* has departed this world, there must remain an active fail-safe *guardian* ready to fulfill this role. No new "software" is needed – the final message has been delivered by Muhammad. Nevertheless, the need to *guard* that message, *interpret* it correctly and *lead* the community according to it persists.

But whose narrative matches up with fact? Whose version of events represents the truth in tact? Which community among those associating with Muhammad is right? Which community is protected by the living *guardian* – whether known publicly or out of sight? A sincere seeker of the truth need not look very far to discover the numerous reports in which the Messenger of God, Muhammad, links the fate of his community with the existence of 12 leaders after him. The most notable records[30] of Muhammad's reported sayings (*ḥadīth*), defended by Muslim groups with conflicting narratives, are actually in resounding agreement on this point. Despite their fundamental differences in matters of creed and legal rulings, these sources confirm that same basic idea about 12 leaders succeeding Muhammad, all of whom hail from Muhammad's tribe. This fact alone leaves no room to doubt that Muhammad indeed relayed that message.

A comparable concurrence[31] applies to the reports in which the last *chosen one* describes how he is leaving behind two weighty things: (1) the Qur'ān and (2) his Ahl al-Bayt (the People of His Household). Many of these reports tell us that the two will not separate from one another. This implies a distinct caliber of impeccable guidance represented by the "Ahl al-Bayt."

Thus, the People of the Household referred to here are not just any blood relative of the Prophet Muhammad. They are pure, impeccable, immaculate *guardians*. As God reveals in the Qur'ān,

إِنَّمَا يُرِيدُ اللَّهُ لِيُذْهِبَ عَنكُمُ الرِّجْسَ أَهْلَ البَيتِ وَيُطَهِّرَكُمْ تَطْهِيرًا

Indeed God desires to repel all impurity from you, O People of the Household, and purify you with a thorough purification.[32]

This will by God is not merely a prescription – for God would want all individuals to stay away from sinful activity, not only Ahl al-Bayt. Specifically addressing Ahl al-Bayt, rather, means that this will is a reality God has actualized in the case of these *guardians*.

By surveying the surviving narratives associated with Prophet Muhammad's Islam, the discerning reader can now realize that only *Twelver Shī'ah Islam* matches up with all these facts (and many others) *seamlessly*. As the Qur'ān helps us to reflect,

أَلَمْ يَأْنِ لِلَّذِينَ آمَنُوا أَن تَخْشَعَ قُلُوبُهُمْ لِذِكْرِ اللَّهِ وَما نَزَلَ
مِنَ الْحَقِّ وَلا يَكُونُوا كَالَّذِينَ أُوتُوا الْكِتابَ مِن قَبْلُ فَطالَ
عَلَيْهِمُ الأَمَدُ فَقَسَتْ قُلُوبُهُمْ ۖ وَكَثِيرٌ مِنْهُم فاسِقُونَ

Is it not time yet for those who have faith that their hearts should be humbled for God's remembrance and to the truth which has come down [to them], and to be not like those who were given the Book before? Time took its toll on them and so their hearts were hardened, and many of them are transgressors.[33]

The Qur'ān Guides to the Guardians

In the very first chapter of the Qur'ān, the Opening chapter (*al-fātiḥah*), we read,

اهْدِنَا الصِّراطَ المُسْتَقِيمَ، صِراطَ الَّذِينَ أَنْعَمْتَ عَلَيْهِم غَيْرِ
المَغْضُوبِ عَلَيْهِم وَلَا الضّالِّينَ

Guide us on the straight path, the path of those whom You have blessed —such as

have not incurred Your wrath, nor are astray.[34]

The Qur'ān, in line with sound reasoning, leads us to expect a path of guidance, one that distinguishes the way of "the blessed" from that of the wretched. So who are the leading figures of this path, "those whom God has blessed," after the last *chosen one*? The Qur'ān has its own way of answering our question clearly. The reference in this Opening Chapter is made and later verses of the Qur'ān pick up the same theme. God says,

وَمَن يُطِعِ اللَّهَ وَالرَّسُولَ فَأُولَٰئِكَ مَعَ الَّذِينَ أَنْعَمَ اللَّهُ عَلَيْهِم مِنَ النَّبِيِّينَ وَالصِّدِّيقِينَ وَالشُّهَدَاءِ وَالصَّالِحِينَ ۚ وَحَسُنَ أُولَٰئِكَ رَفِيقًا

Whoever obeys God and the Messenger — they are with those whom God has blessed, including the prophets and the truthful, the witnesses and the righteous. What excellent companions they are![35]

So, quite clearly, "those whom God has blessed" are not only prophets. They include other saintly figures. What more can the Qur'ān tell us about these personalities of the straight path? The same phrase also appears in this verse of the Qur'ān,

أُولَٰئِكَ الَّذِينَ أَنْعَمَ اللَّهُ عَلَيْهِم مِّنَ النَّبِيِّينَ مِن ذُرِّيَّةِ آدَمَ وَمِمَّن حَمَلْنَا مَعَ نُوحٍ وَمِن ذُرِّيَّةِ إِبْرَاهِيمَ وَإِسْرَائِيلَ وَمِمَّن هَدَيْنَا وَاجْتَبَيْنَا ۚ إِذَا تُتْلَىٰ عَلَيْهِم آيَاتُ الرَّحْمَٰنِ خَرُّوا سُجَّدًا وَبُكِيًّا ۩

They are those whom God has blessed from among the prophets of Adam's progeny, and from [the progeny of] those We carried with Noah, and from among the progeny of Abraham and Israel, and from among those We guided and chose. When the signs of the All-beneficent were recited to them, they would fall down weeping in prostration.[36]

In this verse, there is another reference to "those whom God has blessed" and, apparently not only

prophets – for the prophets of the various proge-
nies are joined by, "those We guided and chose." Is
there a verse in the Qur'ān that identifies this lat-
ter group more specifically? Consider these verses,

وَإِسْمَاعِيلَ وَالْيَسَعَ وَيُونُسَ وَلُوطًا ۚ وَكُلًّا فَضَّلْنَا عَلَى
الْعَالَمِينَ. وَمِنْ آبَائِهِمْ وَذُرِّيَّاتِهِمْ وَإِخْوَانِهِمْ ۖ وَاجْتَبَيْنَاهُمْ
وَهَدَيْنَاهُمْ إِلَىٰ صِرَاطٍ مُسْتَقِيمٍ

and Ishmael, Elisha, Jonah and Lot —each
We graced over all the worlds— and from
among their fathers, their descendants
and brethren —We chose them and guided
them to a straight path[37]

From this verse, there seems to be an indication
that some of the ones guided and chosen by God –
prophets or otherwise – hail from the progeny of
Ishmael (son of Abraham). Recounting a prayer by
Abraham and his son Ishmael, the Qur'ān brings to
light the significance of Ishmael's progeny further,

رَبَّنَا وَاجْعَلْنَا مُسْلِمَيْنِ لَكَ وَمِن ذُرِّيَّتِنَا أُمَّةً مُسْلِمَةً لَّكَ
وَأَرِنَا مَنَاسِكَنَا وَتُبْ عَلَيْنَا ۖ إِنَّكَ أَنتَ التَّوَّابُ الرَّحِيمُ. رَبَّنَا

وَابعَث فيهِم رَسولًا مِنهُم يَتلو عَلَيهِم آياتِكَ وَيُعَلِّمُهُمُ
الكِتابَ وَالحِكمَةَ وَيُزَكّيهِم ۚ إِنَّكَ أَنتَ العَزيزُ الحَكيمُ

*Our Lord, make us submissive to You, and
[raise] from our progeny a community
submissive to You, and show us our rites [of
worship], and turn to us clemently. Indeed
You are the All-clement, the All-merciful.
Our Lord, raise amongst them a Messenger
from among them, who should recite to
them Your signs, and teach them the Book
and wisdom, and purify them. Indeed You
are the All-mighty, the All-wise.'³⁸*

Two prophets, *chosen ones* in their own right, are
asking God to make them "submissive" in this
verse. This intense level of submission must be
one befitting of the impeccable spiritual station
they already enjoy. In the same prayer, they ask
God to elect a group from among their progeny to
have seemingly the same type of submission to
God. Then, Abraham and Ishmael ask that God
raise a Messenger from among this elite spiritual
group. The final Messenger of God, Muhammad,

and the leading members of his household are the most prominent descendants of Abraham through Ishmael. God appears to address this submitting community directly in another verse, saying,

وَجَاهِدوا فِي اللّهِ حَقَّ جِهادِهِ ۚ هُوَ اجتَباكُم وَما جَعَلَ عَلَيكُم فِي الدّينِ مِن حَرَجٍ ۚ مِلَّةَ أَبيكُم إِبراهيمَ ۚ هُوَ سَمّاكُمُ المُسلِمينَ مِن قَبلُ وَفي هذا لِيَكونَ الرَّسولُ شَهيدًا عَلَيكُم وَتَكونوا شُهَداءَ عَلَى النّاسِ ۚ فَأَقيموا الصَّلاةَ وَآتوا الزَّكاةَ وَاعتَصِموا بِاللّهِ هُوَ مَولاكُم ۖ فَنِعمَ المَولى وَنِعمَ النَّصيرُ

And strive for the sake of God, a striving which is worthy of Him. He has chosen you and has not placed for you any hardship in the religion, the faith of your father, Abraham. He named you 'muslims [those submitting to God]' before, and in this, so that the Messenger may be a witness to you, and that you may be witnesses to mankind. So maintain the prayer, give the zakāt [alms], and hold fast to God. He is your master —an excellent master and an ex-cellent helper.[39]

The group being addressed has been chosen for a special station. These individuals are witnesses to the rest of humanity and the Messenger of God is the witness to them. So they are included among "those whom God blessed" in the verse discussed earlier,

وَمَن يُطِعِ اللَّهَ وَالرَّسُولَ فَأُولَٰئِكَ مَعَ الَّذِينَ أَنعَمَ اللَّهُ عَلَيهِم مِنَ النَّبِيِّينَ وَالصِّدِّيقِينَ وَالشُّهَدَاءِ وَالصَّالِحِينَ ۚ وَحَسُنَ أُولَٰئِكَ رَفِيقًا

Whoever obeys God and the Messenger — they are with those whom God has blessed, including the prophets and the truthful, the witnesses and the righteous. What ex-cellent companions they are![40]

The Qur'ān describes the special group from Abra-ham's progeny as one envied for its merits,

أَمْ يَحْسُدُونَ النَّاسَ عَلَىٰ مَا آتَاهُمُ اللَّهُ مِن فَضْلِهِ فَقَدْ آتَيْنَا آلَ إِبْرَاهِيمَ الْكِتَابَ وَالْحِكْمَةَ وَآتَيْنَاهُم مُّلْكًا عَظِيمًا

Or do they envy the people for what God has given them out of His grace? We have certainly given the progeny of Abraham the Book and wisdom, and We have given them a great sovereignty.[41]

That great sovereignty is the vested authority of the *guardian Imams*. It is the Imamate, the leadership that Prophet Abraham was granted after being tested. God made it clear to Abraham that the wrongdoers among his progeny could not become Imams. As the Qur'ān relates,

وَإِذِ ابْتَلَىٰ إِبْرَاهِيمَ رَبُّهُ بِكَلِمَاتٍ فَأَتَمَّهُنَّ قَالَ إِنِّي جَاعِلُكَ لِلنَّاسِ إِمَامًا قَالَ وَمِن ذُرِّيَّتِي قَالَ لَا يَنَالُ عَهْدِي الظَّالِمِينَ

And when his Lord tested Abraham with certain words, and he fulfilled them, He

said, 'I am making you the Imam of man-kind.' Said he, 'And from among my descendants?' He said, 'My pledge does not extend to the unjust.'[42]

The 12 Imams who succeed Prophet Muhammad are mentioned in the Qur'ān, if only we read properly. Their attributes are cross-referenced in the stories of faith communities throughout the Qur'ān. Although this short booklet can only offer a glimpse, we may find comfort reflecting upon God's following assurance,

وَنُرِيدُ أَن نَّمُنَّ عَلَى الَّذِينَ اسْتُضْعِفُوا فِي الأَرْضِ وَنَجْعَلَهُمْ

أَئِمَّةً وَنَجْعَلَهُمُ الوارِثِينَ

And We desire to show favor to those who were oppressed in the land, and to make them imams, and to make them the heirs[43]

The Imam is Our Guardian

God protects a *guardian*, and the *guardian* is ever-ready to fulfill his roles, but people's evil choices or ill preparation can prevent them from experiencing the full range of a *guardian*'s benefits. As the Qur'ān teaches,

وَلَو أَنَّ أَهلَ القُرىٰ آمَنوا وَاتَّقَوا لَفَتَحنا عَلَيِهم بَرَكاتٍ مِنَ السَّماءِ وَالأَرضِ وَلَكِن كَذَّبوا فَأَخَذناهُم بِما كانوا يَكسِبونَ

If the people of the towns had been faithful and Godwary, We would have opened to them blessings from the heaven and the earth. But they denied; so We seized them because of what they used to earn.[44]

The failings of evil-doers can have far-reaching impacts on us all. For that, the blame lies on the shoulders of those betraying the will of God. Having said that, we also have a responsibility to share the truth, promote virtue and prevent vice to the best of our ability, as the circumstances permit.

If human failures force the *guardian* to tactically retreat behind the scenes, reference to the upright scholars of the *guarded community* remains in line with intuitive sense and is the expected recourse unless the living *guardian* instructs otherwise. As the Qur'ān says,

وَما كانَ الْمُؤمِنونَ لِيَنفِروا كافَّةً ۚ فَلَولا نَفَرَ مِن كُلِّ فِرقَةٍ مِنهُم طائِفَةٌ لِيَتَفَقَّهوا فِي الدّينِ وَلِيُنذِروا قَومَهُم إِذا رَجَعوا إِلَيهِم لَعَلَّهُم يَحذَرونَ

Yet it is not for the faithful to go forth en masse. But why should not there go forth a group from each of their sections to become learned in religion, and to warn their people when they return to them, so that they may beware?[45]

Thus, there are scholars that specialize and to whom non-specialists refer in matters of their religious conduct. If such scholars agree in their understanding, then people can refer to any one of them. But if these scholars disagree, sound reasoning dictates that the non-expert should refer to the most qualified expert among them.[46] For, in this case of disagreement, a person is sure that referring to the most qualified individual among them is permitted but is unsure whether referring to others is equally prescribed. A reasonable individual should, then, elect the surely excusable choice. What justifies referring to scholars that might err? Even though these upright scholarly reference points can potentially err, following them is certainly excusable so long as the *living* Imam sanctions it. The impeccable *guardian*, ready to intervene by God's command – typically through ordinary means, and miraculously if necessary – guarantees that the *guarded community* is heading in the right direction. For those treading the path of sound reasoning and following the guidance of Muhammad, God promises,

وَالَّذِينَ جَاهَدوا فِينا لَنَهْدِيَنَّهُم سُبُلَنا ۚ وَإِنَّ اللَّهَ لَمَعَ المُحسِنينَ

As for those who strive for Us, We shall surely guide them in Our ways, and God is indeed with the virtuous.[47]

NOTES

[1] References are particularly due to lectures and works by:

- S. Muḥammad Ḥusayn al-Ṭabāṭabāʾī
- Sh. Murtaḍá al-Muṭahharī
- S. Muḥammad Bāqir al-Ṣadr
- Sh. Ghulām Riḍā al-Fayyāḍī
- Sh. Nāṣir Makārim al-Shīrāzī
- Sh. Jaʿfar al-Subḥānī
- S. Jaʿfar al-Ḥakīm
- S. Munīr al-Khabbāz
- S. Muḥammad Bāqir al-Sīstānī
- S. Muḥammad ʿAlī Baḥr al-ʿulūm
- S. Sāmī al-Badrī
- S. Muḥammad Rizvī

[2] Attributed to ʿAlī ibn al-Ḥusayn, known as Zayn al-ʿābidīn, Munājāt al-Shākirīn

[3] See the previous booklets in this series

Provided that it is needed for knowing who the *chosen ones* and *guardians* are, as that would make it part of the threshold of truth protected in every age. The wisdom of the one with no need dictates that the purpose of human excellence be achieved and the excellent *guardian* survive to guide and safeguard.

(See this note after reading the entire booklet) Translation is almost necessarily an act of interpretation, albeit one of varying degrees. Sometimes differences in translation do not reflect an essentially different meaning, but can present more suitable alternatives given the target reader's background. This is one of the reasons why the original Arabic should be reviewed when attempting to make less obvious claims about the meaning of verses, and even words, in the Qur'ān. In referencing the many straightforward verses in this short booklet, I have benefitted from Qarai's translation, with some modifications. As expected, the Qur'ān is accessible in its straightforward verses and through clear cross-referencing in at least some verses. But the Qur'ān has its guardians that can explain the less straightforward verses and clarify depths of meaning in the entire Qur'ān. When no direct access to such a guardian is available, due to human shortcomings, reference to the upright scholars of the *guarded community* is the next best option. Hence, for verses requiring closer examination, the reader is advised to review several different translation attempts to get a sense of the varied interpretation. Rather, a reader should not be satisfied with mere translation attempts, and should consult the exegesis literature, in order to be reasonably sure before making a claim about a given verse's meaning. This is not to say we cannot contemplate and reflect on meaningful interpretation possibilities. A reader may also realize how the pensive recitation of such verses, despite interpretation differences, can help instill a more profound connection to ideas we already know to be true, regardless what new knowledge the verses aim to convey.

[6] Qur'ān 17:88

[7] Qur'ān 21:30

[8] Qur'ān 51:47

[9] Qur'ān 27:88

[10] Qur'ān 41:53

[11] Qur'ān 17:9

[12] Qur'ān 11:13-14

[13] Qur'ān 10:38

[14] Qur'ān 33:21

[15] Qur'ān 68:4

[16] Qur'ān 33:40-48

[17] Qur'ān 29:48

[18] Muhammad

[19] Qur'ān 53:2-4

[20] Qur'ān 7:157

[21] Even putting aside matters of mistranslation or tampering, however, some words or phrases in those scriptures may have been passed down in an adulterated form due to scribal errors, for example.

[22] Qur'ān 34:28

[23] Qur'ān 21:107

[24] Qur'ān 3:31

[25] Qur'ān 35:15

[26] Qur'ān 8:24

[27] Qur'ān 24:54

[28] Qur'ān 3:144

[29] Qur'ān 4:59

[30] See the major ḥadīth collections of both the Sunnīs (e.g. Ṣaḥīḥ al-Bukhārī, Ṣaḥīḥ Muslim, Sunan Abī Dāwūd, Sunan al-Tirmidhī, Musnad Aḥmad...) and the Shīʿīs (e.g. al-Kāfī)

[31] See the major ḥadīth collections of both the Sunnīs (e.g. Ṣaḥīḥ Muslim, Mustadrak al-Ḥākim al-Nīsābūrī, Sunan al-Tirmidhī, Musnad Aḥmad...) and the Shīʿīs (e.g. al-Kāfī)

[32] Qur'ān 33:33

[33] Qur'ān 57:16

[34] Qur'ān 1:6-7

[35] Qur'ān 4:69

[36] Qur'ān 19:58

[37] Qur'ān 6:86-87

[38] Qur'ān 2:128-129

[39] Qur'ān 22:78

[40] Qur'ān 4:69

[41] Qur'ān 4:54

[42] Qur'ān 2:124

[43] Qur'ān 28:5

[44] Qur'ān 7:96

[45] Qur'ān 9:122

[46] Unless the most qualified expert has concluded that any expert opinion suffices. If one prefers to take precaution then that requires knowledge of how to take precaution and precaution is

not always possible (that is, a person may be stuck between a rock and a hard place). The most qualified scholar(s) of the *guarded community* can clarify the guidelines.

[47] Qur'ān 29:69

www.ingramcontent.com/pod-product-compliance
Lightning Source LLC
Chambersburg PA
CBHW020521030426
42337CB00011B/495